IT'S TIME TO LEARN ABOUT ANTELOPES

It's Time to Learn about Antelopes

Walter the Educator

Silent King Books
A WhichHead Entertainment Imprint

Copyright © 2025 by Walter the Educator

All rights reserved. No part of this book may be reproduced in any manner whatsoever without written per- mission except in the case of brief quotations embodied in critical articles and reviews.

First Printing, 2024

Disclaimer

This book is a literary work; the story is not about specific persons, locations, situations, and/or circumstances unless mentioned in a historical context. Any resemblance to real persons, locations, situations, and/or circumstances is coincidental. This book is for entertainment and informational purposes only. The author and publisher offer this information without warranties expressed or implied. No matter the grounds, neither the author nor the publisher will be accountable for any losses, injuries, or other damages caused by the reader's use of this book. The use of this book acknowledges an understanding and acceptance of this disclaimer.

It's Time to Learn about Antelopes is a collectible early learning book by Walter the Educator suitable for all ages belonging to Walter the Educator's Time to Eat Book Series. Collect more books at WaltertheEducator.com

USE THE EXTRA SPACE TO TAKE NOTES AND DOCUMENT YOUR MEMORIES

ANTELOPES

The antelope is fast and free,

It's Time to Learn about Antelopes

Running wild where grasslands be.

With hooves so light and legs so strong,

It sprints and leaps the whole day long!

Its body's sleek, its fur is neat,

With colors brown and white so sweet.

Some have spots, and some have stripes,

Each one special, bold, and bright!

On top its head, what do we see?

Two strong horns as tall as trees!

Some twist and curl, some point up high,

Helping them as years go by.

They live in herds, both big and small,

Together safe, watching all.

If danger's near, they stomp and dash,

Speeding off in a mighty flash!

It's Time to Learn about
Antelopes

Grass and leaves are what they eat,

Crunching plants so green and sweet.

Nibbling here, munching there,

Finding food most everywhere!

With ears so big, they hear so well,

A tiny sound, oh, they can tell!

They twitch and turn, they always know,

If a sneaky threat is low.

From deserts dry to forests wide,

In open fields they run and hide.

Across the plains, through trees so tall,

Antelopes can live through all!

Moms take care of babies small,

Hiding them in grasses tall.

Soon they stand and start to play,

It's Time to Learn about Antelopes

Then they run so fast one day!

Cousins near, but not the same,

Gazelles and kudus share their name.

Springboks leap and pronghorns glide,

All with beauty, speed, and pride!

So now you know this gentle friend,

With legs that jump and horns that bend.

The antelope so quick and bright,

It's Time to Learn about
Antelopes

A wondrous creature, what a sight!

ABOUT THE CREATOR

Walter the Educator is one of the pseudonyms for Walter Anderson. Formally educated in Chemistry, Business, and Education, he is an educator, an author, a diverse entrepreneur, and he is the son of a disabled war veteran. "Walter the Educator" shares his time between educating and creating. He holds interests and owns several creative projects that entertain, enlighten, enhance, and educate, hoping to inspire and motivate you. Follow, find new works, and stay up to date with Walter the Educator™

at WaltertheEducator.com

www.ingramcontent.com/pod-product-compliance
Lightning Source LLC
LaVergne TN
LVHW052017060526
838201LV00059B/4063